KINGDOM CLASSIFICATION

SUNFLOWERS, MAGNOLIA TREES & OTHER
FLOWERING PLANTS

BY STEVE PARKER

First published in the United States in 2009 by
Compass Point Books
151 Good Counsel Drive
P.O. Box 669
Mankato, MN 56002-0669

KINGDOM CLASSIFICATION—FLOWERING PLANTS
was produced by

David West Children's Books
7 Princeton Court
55 Felsham Road
London SW15 1AZ

 This book was manufactured with paper containing
at least 10 percent post-consumer waste.

Designer: Rob Shone
Editors: Gail Bushnell, Anthony Wacholtz
Page Production: Bobbie Nuytten

Creative Director: Joe Ewest
Art Director: LuAnn Ascheman-Adams
Editorial Director: Nick Healy
Managing Editor: Catherine Neitge

Library of Congress Cataloging-in-Publication Data
Parker, Steve, 1952–
   Sunflowers, magnolia trees & other flowering plants / by
Steve Parker.
       p. cm.—(Kingdom classifications)
   Includes index.
   ISBN 978-0-7565-4222-1 (library binding)
 1. Angiosperms—Juvenile literature. 2. Flowers—Juvenile
literature. I. Parker, Steve, 1952– Kingdom classifications
II. Title. III. Title: Sunflowers, magnolia trees and other
flowering plants. IV. Series.
   QK495.A1P37 2009
   582.13—dc22   2009013696

Visit Compass Point Books on the Internet at
www.compasspointbooks.com
or e-mail your request to
custserv@compasspointbooks.com

Front cover: Passion flower
Opposite: Calendula arvensis

SUNFLOWERS, MAGNOLIA TREES & OTHER
FLOWERING PLANTS

Steve Parker

Compass Point Books ✦ Minneapolis, Minnesota

TABLE OF CONTENTS

INTRODUCTION	6	WORLD OF FLOWERS	18
WHAT ARE FLOWERING PLANTS?	8	POLLINATION	20
HOW FLOWERS BEGAN	10	FRUITS AND SEEDS	22
PARTS OF A PLANT	12	ONE COT OR TWO?	24
SOLAR POWER	14	FROM SEED TO SEEDLING	26
BUSHES AND TREES	16	OUT IN THE COLD	28

WOODS AND FORESTS 30

GRASSLANDS 32

WETLAND PLANTS 34

DESERTS AND DROUGHTS 36

PLANT PRODUCTS 38

THE FLOWER BUSINESS 40

FLOWERS UNDER THREAT 42

CLASSIFICATION OF LIFE 44

GROUPS OF FLOWERING PLANTS 45

GLOSSARY 46

FURTHER RESOURCES 47

INDEX 48

Almost everywhere we look, we see flowering plants. They may not have flowers, fruits, seeds, or even leaves—like a bare tree in the winter. But the flowering plants, known as angiosperms, live in almost every land habitat besides the coldest regions at the poles and the highest mountains.

With almost 300,000 species, flowering plants are by far the most common and widespread group of plants around the world. They vary from delicate herbs and wildflowers to large broad-leaved trees. They are food for herbivorous (plant-eating) animals, from caterpillars to elephants. As farm crops, they provide the bulk of our own food. And they brighten our lives with their color and beauty.

BEAUTIFUL BLOSSOM

*All flowering plants have flowers,
which produce seeds. When a tree is
in blossom, it has produced its
flowers. Cherry trees blossom in the
spring, with a wonderful display of
hundreds of bright flowers.*

WHAT ARE FLOWERING PLANTS?

All flowering plants have flowers at some stage in their lives. The flowers are the parts used to reproduce by making seeds that will grow into new plants.

FABULOUS FLOWERS

Flowers are all around us. Bluebells (1) carpet woods in the spring. Cactus flowers (2) appear every several years. Pampas grass flowers (3) are soft and fluffy. Almond blossoms (4) appear before the tree's leaves. The lotus (5) is worshipped in some regions. The banana flower (6) can be eaten as a vegetable or left to develop into bananas.

THE ROLE OF FLOWERS

The basic parts of a flowering plant are its roots, an upright stem, green leaves, and flowers. Seeds develop inside the flowers. The seeds are covered by various layers, including the hard case around a nut seed and the fleshy fruit around an apple pip seed. The name *angiosperm* means "enclosed or hidden seed." Other plants make seeds, too. But the seeds of those plants are not enclosed.

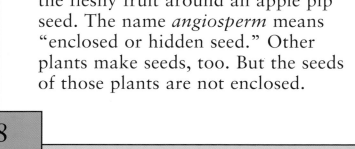

CYCLE OF LIFE

Some flowering plants have flowers all year. But most only produce flowers at a certain time, often in the spring or the summer, when growing conditions are best. Many flowers have colorful parts, especially the petals. Some flowers can grow as large as your head. Others are small and pale green or brown. Grasses are flowering plants, but their flowers are much less colorful. Most look feathery or are brushlike.

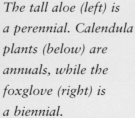

ANNUALS, BIENNIALS, AND PERENNIALS

Annuals are flowering plants that grow from seeds, produce flowers and seeds, and die within a year. Those that take two years for this life cycle—growing in the first year and then producing flowers and seeds in the second—are called biennials. Flowering plants that continue to grow and flower year after year, such as trees, bushes, and shrubs, are called perennials.

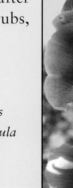

The tall aloe (left) is a perennial. Calendula plants (below) are annuals, while the foxglove (right) is a biennial.

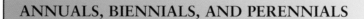

9

HOW FLOWERS BEGAN

The first flowering plants may have appeared on Earth more than 150 million years ago. The world was very different then. Other kinds of plants ruled the land, and dinosaurs roamed among them.

FOSSIL POLLEN

We know about prehistoric life from fossils—hard parts or impressions of living things preserved in rocks. Soft, delicate flowers rarely leave fossils. But bark, seeds, and other hard parts have been preserved or imprinted—especially their tiny pollen grains. Each plant has its own size and shape of pollen grains.

BEFORE FLOWERS

Before the angiosperms arrived, the main plants included conifer trees, ginkgos, cycads (which look like stumpy palm trees), and tall ferns and tree ferns. Conifers formed vast forests and were food for many animals.

FOSSIL FLOWER

The soft parts of flowers can be preserved as fossils, but only in unusual conditions. One example is when a flower falls onto a riverbank and is quickly covered in mud. Florissantia lived from 30 million to 45 million years ago. Fossils of its flowers, pollen, and fruits have been found in western North America.

FRESH LANDSCAPE

Ancient conifers and other plants were mostly green and brown. As flowering plants began to spread, they brought new shapes and colors to the landscape. Various insects, dinosaurs, and other animals that had only eaten meat began to eat the flowers.

CRETACEOUS PLANTS

Flowering plants began to spread during the Cretaceous period (65 million to 145 million years ago). By the period's end, as Tyrannosaurus prowled the land, the scenery had many new kinds of flowers, herbs, bushes, and trees.

OLD FLOWERS

The earliest known fossil flowers include a tiny plant similar to duckweed that dates back 125 million years. Relatives of today's magnolias (left) were thriving in many regions 100 million years ago.

AMBORELLA

The small shrub Amborella trichopoda *(above) may be similar to flowering plants of more than 140 million years ago. It is found east of Australia on the island of New Caledonia. Its pale pink and green flowers have simple inner structures.*

THE RISE OF INSECTS

Today most parts of flowering plants are eaten by insects. Insects also carry the pollen or seeds of many flowers. Insects existed well before flowering plants appeared. As flowers became more common and varied, insects had new sources of food. So new species of insects appeared, including butterflies, moths, flies, bees, wasps, and ants.

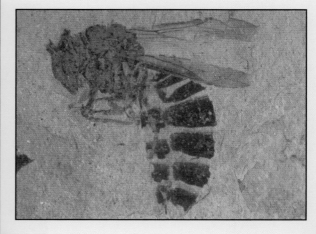

PARTS OF A PLANT

A typical flowering plant has four main parts: roots, stem, leaves, and flowers. Each part besides the flowers plays a certain role in keeping the plant alive and healthy.

VARIATIONS

Some flowering plants have a single upright stem, while others have several growing up from the same place. Large plants, such as trees, might have a million leaves, while small plants might have only one or two.

LEAF

Leaves are like green "solar panels" that take in the energy of sunlight to make the plant's food.

PETIOLE

The petiole is the stalk of a leaf that holds tiny tubes carrying sap and water.

STEM

The main stem is usually stiff and upright. It keeps the flower away from the ground and up in the sunlight. Some plants have horizontal stems, known as creeping stems.

ROOTS

The roots hold the plant in the soil and take in water and minerals. Some plants have a main root called the taproot with others branching from it. Others have lots of small roots.

FLOWER

Flowers are not vital for the plant's survival, but they are essential for the plant to reproduce. Some plants have only one flower, while others have many flowers that make up a group called an inflorescence.

PEDICEL

The pedicel is the stalk of the flower, which contains tiny tubelike vessels that carry water and sap.

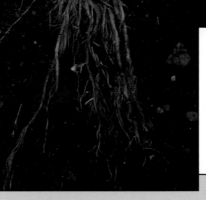

VESSELS

A microscopic view shows tiny vessels carrying water and sap inside a walnut leaf. They are usually grouped together and are known as vascular bundles.

ROOT HAIRS

Large roots have smaller branches called rootlets. The tips of these are covered with thousands of delicate microscopic hairs. Water and minerals are absorbed by these smaller hairs—not the large main roots.

ROOTS

A plant's roots spread out into the soil to give the plant a firm base. Some trees' roots below the ground are as wide as the tree's branches.

PLANT PLUMBING

In the same way that the human body has a network of blood vessels, a network of microscopic tubes spreads to all parts of a flowering plant. The xylem vessels take in water and minerals from the soil and carry them up to the leaves. The phloem vessels transport energy-rich sap made by the leaves to the other parts of the plant.

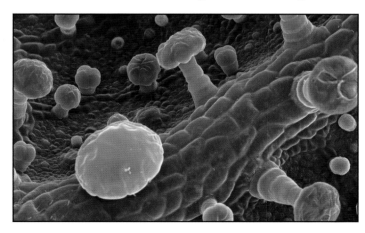

LEAF HAIRS

Many leaves have tiny, hairlike structures called trichomes, especially on the underside (above, on a walnut leaf). They help prevent moisture from being lost inside the leaf.

TUBERS AND CORMS

Various plant parts store food to last through winter. Stem tubers are wide, enlarged regions of the stem that hold nutrients, such as starch. Corms are enlarged stems covered by thin, scale-like leaves. A bulb is a short stem with layers of thickened leaves around it to store the food.

The potato (above) is a starchy stem tuber. The crocus "bulb" (right) is a corm, not a true bulb.

13

SOLAR POWER

P lants make their own food from minerals and other substances. They capture energy from the sun during a process called photosynthesis.

THE IMPORTANCE OF LEAVES

While animals get their food by eating and breaking down complex substances in their food, plants create their own food from simple substances. Plants are autotrophs—self-feeding plants. In most flowering plants, leaves capture sunlight to make food. However, some plants, such as cacti, do this in the stem. Others carry it out in parts of the flower or roots.

LOTS OF LEAVES

Each species of plant has its own shape and size of leaf. The palm tree (1) has an umbrella-shaped topping of long leaves, each with many ribbonlike strips. Croton (2) has multicolored leaves in shades of green, yellow, and red. Duckweed (3) can have large or tiny rounded leaves. In the prickly pear cactus (4), the green parts are stems, not leaves. Gunnera (giant rhubarb) leaves (5) are huge. The leaves of the common fig (6) are rough on top but soft and hairy underneath.

14

USING LIGHT

Using light energy to make food is called photosynthesis. The light energy joins with carbon dioxide from the air and water taken up by the roots. This creates high-energy, sugary substances that are carried around the plant as sap.

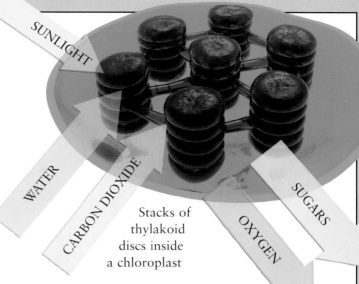

SUNLIGHT

WATER

CARBON DIOXIDE

OXYGEN

SUGARS

Stacks of thylakoid discs inside a chloroplast

PHOTOSYNTHESIS

Photosynthesis occurs in tiny, green blobs called chloroplasts in the cells of leaves. It produces oxygen as a waste product, which is useful because animals (including humans) must breathe this gas to survive.

EXTRA LIGHT

Lithops have unusually thick leaves with see-through "windows" on top to let in extra light. The leaves are at ground level on a very short stem and often have to grow in the shade of taller plants.

STOMATA

A leaf has tiny holes, stomata, especially in its underside. Through these holes, carbon dioxide enters the plant and oxygen leaves it.

PARASITIC PLANTS

A few species of flowering plants do not make their own food—they steal it. They are parasites—they get food and other needs from another living thing, the host. Since parasitic plants do not carry out photosynthesis, they lack colored substances called pigments, especially green chlorophyll, that trap light energy. Because they don't use photosynthesis to get food, they can grow in the shade.

The ghost plant is a parasite on fungi (molds) growing in the soil beneath it.

The biggest flowering plants are bushes, shrubs, and trees. They are woody, meaning their main stems—their trunks—and their branches are made of tough substances, such as lignin. This holds up the plants.

OAK FLOWERS

Oak trees have pale male flowers called catkins. The female flowers are much smaller and are easily overlooked.

DECIDUOUS TREES

Most angiosperm trees and bushes are deciduous—they lose their leaves at a certain time, usually during the winter or the dry season. In an oak tree, the new, soft leaves come out in the spring and are pale green (1). In the summer, they become tougher and darker (2). In the fall, they turn yellow or brown, die, and begin to drop (3).

In the winter, the branches are bare (4).

TRUNKS, BRANCHES, AND TWIGS

Branches grow from the trunk, and twigs, which are smaller, grow from the branches. The trunk, branches, and twigs grow each year. A tree gets taller as it ages, but it also thickens. Some angiosperm trees are more than 2,000 years old.

HORSE CHESTNUT CANDLES

Tree flowers, called blossoms, are often described by their similarity to other objects. Horse chestnut flowers are sometimes known as candles, spikes, or pyramids from their tall, upright, tapering shape.

WHICH IS WHICH?

A tree is usually a tall plant with a strong, woody trunk, from which branches grow outward. A bush or shrub tends to be lower, usually less than 16 feet (5 meters) tall. Bushes have many branches growing up from the ground.

INSIDE A TREE TRUNK

Under the protective outer bark is phloem (inner bark), with thousands of microscopic vessels that carry nutrient-rich sap from the leaves to other parts. Xylem (sapwood) vessels transport water and minerals up from the roots. Between these two layers is thin cambium, which makes new phloem and xylem.

Outer bark
Phloem layer
Cambium layer
Xylem layer
Growth rings

Heartwood

SPREADING SHRUBS

The term "shrubby habit" describes a bush or shrub, such as the rhododendron (below), that stays low and spreads as a tangle of branches. Some plants can grow as either shrubs or trees, depending on the type of soil, rainfall, and other conditions.

SHOWY BLOSSOMS

Compared with oak flowers, cherry blossoms (right) are big and bright. Many species of cherry trees have been bred for their beautiful white and pink blossoms.

DENDROLOGY

The study of trees is called dendrology. Each year a tree grows, it forms a new light and dark layer called a growth ring beneath its bark. The number of rings shows the tree's age. The rings also give clues to the weather and climate in the past. A thick, light ring is proof of a spring with good growing conditions.

A drill-like device removes a section of wood for analysis.

WORLD OF FLOWERS

The main purpose of a flower is to produce seeds so the plant can continue its life cycle. However, flowers have several ways of doing this, as shown by their amazing variety in size, shape, and color.

BUDS

A bud is a small, lumpy part containing a new shoot or flower inside a covering of small leaves that protect it. Sunflowers (top) start to grow from the leaves of buds (above).

FEMALE AND MALE

Flowers are the plant's reproductive parts. Some have both female and male breeding structures and are known as bisexual or perfect flowers. Other flowers have only female or male parts and are called unisexual. An individual plant with both male and female flowers is monoecious. A plant with only female or male flowers is dioecious.

FLOWER VARIETY

A rainbow tree (left) has petals of various colors on different flowers. The passionflower (above left) has five pale sepals and five petals that look similar. The globe artichoke (right) has pointed outer parts and thin, purple inner ones.

18

SEPALS

Sepals are the flower's outermost parts. They are often green and not very noticeable. In a daffodil (right), they are large and yellow, resembling petals. The darker yellow petals come together to form a trumpet-shaped corolla.

INSIDE A FLOWER

In a hellebore flower (below), the stamens have baglike anthers that contain pollen grains. Each anther is at the end of a long stalk, the filament. The carpels are the stigma, the inner tip of the flower, which is on a long style above the ovary and ovules.

Sepal
Petal
Anther
Filament
Stigma
Style
Ovary
Ovules
Receptacle

FLOWER PARTS

A typical flower has four main sets of parts. On the outside is a layer of pale sepals. Underneath is a layer of petals, which are often large and colorful. The male parts (the stamens) and female parts (the carpels) are at the center of the flower.

FLOWER SIZE

Flowers range in size, from being as tiny as the dot on this "i" to as big as a person. Among the smallest are the flowers of duckweeds and watermeals—floating plants found in ponds and slow rivers. The largest single flower is rafflesia, measuring almost 3 feet (1 m) across. The titan arum is the biggest inflorescence (group of flowers on a stalk).

The titan arum (far left) can grow to be 10 feet (3 m) tall. Rafflesia (left) is much bigger than wolffia watermeal (below).

POLLINATION

Flowers make seeds, but only after the plants have been pollinated. This involves transferring tiny pollen grains from the male parts to the female parts.

POLLEN AND EGGS

Pollen grains contain microscopic male sex cells, called gametes or sperm. These cells fertilize the female gametes, which are called eggs. Only then can the fertilized eggs start to grow and form seeds.

MAMMALS

Animal-pollinated flowers usually have bright colors, strong scents, and sweet nectar to attract animals. Pollinating mammals include mice, voles, and bats (below).

POLLEN GRAINS

Pollen grains are formed in the anthers, which split to release them. For pollination they must reach the stigma. Then each grain grows a long pollen tube down the style to the ovary. The male cells pass through this tube to reach the female cells.

BIRDS

Hummingbirds (right) are among many birds attracted to the sweet nectar. The pollen from the anthers brushes onto the birds' bodies, and pollen from previous flowers brushes off onto the stigma.

INSECTS

Among the insects that carry pollen are bees (above), wasps, ants, beetles, butterflies, moths, and flies. Apart from the sugary nectar, they also eat the pollen, but there are usually thousands of grains left over.

EELGRASS

Only a few plants use water for pollination, such as the marine eelgrass *Zostera marina*. The grains float in water currents from one flower to another. Eelgrass is also one of the few flowering plants found in salty water. Most water-dwelling plants live in freshwater.

Marine eelgrass grows in shallow coastal water.

WIND POLLINATION

Flowers such as hazel catkins (left) use air currents to transfer their pollen. Their pollen grains are very light and may have flaps that catch the breeze.

HELP FROM US

Plant breeders do not leave pollination to chance. To keep flower features they want, they gather pollen from selected flowers using a paintbrush (right). Then they wipe it onto the female parts of other chosen flowers.

METHODS

Pollen can be moved by wind, animals, or water. Usually it only fertilizes the eggs in flowers of the same species. In a flower with both male and female parts, the pollen is usually released before the female parts are ready to be fertilized.

LOOK-ALIKE

Some flowers trick animals into helping them with pollination. The bee orchid (left) looks similar to a female bee. Male bees try to mate with the flower, picking up pollen to take to another flower.

FRUITS AND SEEDS

After pollination and fertilization, the flower develops its seeds. These are enclosed within the ovary—the key feature of flowering plants.

READY TO GROW

The fertilized egg cell begins by multiplying into two cells. Those cells divide into four cells, which divide into eight, and so on. Soon there are millions of cells, which form a tiny plant called an embryo. The embryo is contained in a tough case that holds food for growth. The embryo, food, and case are called a seed.

FRUIT MARKET

Many kinds of fruits, which all contain seeds, are commonly known as vegetables. They include cucumbers, tomatoes, peas, beans, peppers, squash, and corn.

VARIETY OF FRUITS

Shell ginger is a tropical plant that produces round fruits with ridges (above). Grass seeds are actually tiny fruits with thin outer layers (left). Acorns (below left) are the fruits of oak trees. Palm fruits (below) change color as they ripen.

SEED PODS

In plants such as peas, beans, and the siris tree, seeds form in long containers called pods. In the siris tree (right), the pods are 8 inches (20 cm) long. They gradually dry and burst to release the seeds.

TROPICAL

A fruit forms around a seed from the ovary in the base of the flower. There are many kinds of fruits. The type of fruit is determined by which parts of the ovary and nearby tissues grow and ripen. Various kinds of berries and nuts are fruits. Of course, apples, pears, and pineapples are fruits as well.

INSIDE A SEED

Most seeds have a strong outer casing, the testa, to prevent damage and drying out. Underneath is the endocarp layer, which is also protective. The embryo plant begins to develop its first shoots, the epicotyl and plumule, and its first root, the radicle. As it starts to germinate, its food for the first days or weeks is stored in the cotyledons.

BIGGEST FRUIT

The largest fruit is the coco-de-mer. It grows on a type of palm tree on islands in the Indian Ocean. The fruit takes six years to ripen. It can grow up to 20 inches (50 cm) in length and weigh 66 pounds (30 kilograms).

MANY SEEDS

A lotus flower seed head has nutlike seeds (left). A strawberry (right) is a "false fruit" because the flesh does not come from the ovary.

Testa (seed coat)

Endocarp

Radicle (root)

Hypocotyl (shoot)

Cotyledon

VEGETATIVE GROWTH

Vegetative propagation is a form of reproduction that does not involve pollen or seeds. The plant grows special shoots, stems, or roots, from which new plants develop. This is a form of asexual reproduction. The offspring are clones—they have the same genes as the parent plant.

The spider plant produces new "babies" at the ends of stems called stolons.

ONE COT OR TWO?

The parts of flowering plants that store food in seeds are known as cotyledons. Angiosperms are divided into two groups according to the number of cotyledons.

LEAVES

As the castor bean plant grows, its two cotyledons emerge from the seed on a stem and form "seed leaves" that begin photosynthesis. They have smooth, rounded edges, unlike the true leaves, which have deep indentations.

MONO AND DI

Monocots are plants that have one cotyledon per seed, while dicots have two cotyledons in each seed. Grasses, rushes, palm trees, irises, lilies, sweet flags, tulips, bluebells, hyacinths, agaves, yuccas, onions, and garlic are monocots.

THE EXOTIC ORCHIDS

Orchids are not only the largest group of monocots —they are also the largest family of all flowering plants, with more than 20,000 species. They have beautiful, intricate shapes and are found in most habitats, especially tropical forests. Most orchid flowers have three sepals and three petals. The central petal, called the labellum, is often enlarged, making a suitable platform for insects to land on during pollination.

The crimson cattleya orchid grows in northeastern Brazil.

CONTRASTING LEAVES

In the leaves of monocots, such as the carludovica (above left), the veins (ridges) run alongside each other, a pattern known as parallel venation. In dicot leaves, such as in the giant rhubarb (above right), the veins branch and join, an arrangement known as net venation.

LEAVES AND FLOWERS

Monocots have leaves with parallel stripelike veins, which are called vascular bundles. Dicot leaves have branching veins. Monocot flowers have parts in multiples of three, while dicots have parts that usually come in fours or fives.

FLOWERS

The allium family of monocots (above) includes onions, shallots, leeks, and chives, Each has a distinct smell and taste. The ball-shaped flowers have petals and sepals in sets of three, unlike dicots, such as roses (left).

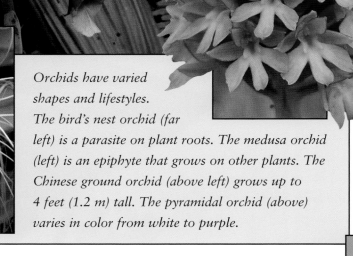

Orchids have varied shapes and lifestyles. The bird's nest orchid (far left) is a parasite on plant roots. The medusa orchid (left) is an epiphyte that grows on other plants. The Chinese ground orchid (above left) grows up to 4 feet (1.2 m) tall. The pyramidal orchid (above) varies in color from white to purple.

FROM SEED TO SEEDLING

The seeds of flowering plants can stay inactive for many years. The embryo plant inside only starts to grow into a seedling when conditions are good.

HELICOPTERS

Maple, sycamore, and ash fruits have long, thin, papery wings and are known as samaras or keys. They change from green to brown as they ripen. They twirl around as they are blown by the wind. This helps the seeds move away from the parent tree.

SPREADING SEEDS

For the most part, it is not good for a seed to fall to the ground next to its parent plant. If it germinates, it will have to compete with the parent for water, soil minerals, and sunlight. To avoid this problem, seeds spread to new areas where there may be open ground with enough space, water, minerals, and light to grow.

Some seeds are dispersed by the wind. Their fruits are usually lightweight and have flaps, wings, or sails. Other seeds are specialized for animal dispersal. Their fruits often have tasty flesh that encourages animals to eat them. The seeds inside are not digested and pass out in the animal's droppings.

PARACHUTES

Dandelions, thistles, and similar plants have fruits with parachute or umbrella shapes. The fruits have woolly hairs and can blow in the wind for hours, usually ending up far away from the main plant.

BERRIES

Many animals, including elephants, squirrels, mice, and birds, feed on berries and other fruits. The tough seeds are unharmed.

PARTS OF A SEEDLING

The cotyledons of a new flowering plant may stay in the soil or be raised on a stalk to work as leaves. The plumule is the first true shoot that sends up leaves at its tip to start photosynthesis. The first root is the radicle, which develops into a network of roots.

First leaves

Plumule

Seed body

Radicle

Tap root

Side roots

GERMINATION

Most seeds germinate in conditions of warmth, moisture, and darkness —commonly in spring soil. Some need a cold shock, known as cold stratification, to begin germination. This is usually provided by winter weather. Others germinate only after being scorched by fire.

HOT SHOCK

Snowbrush ceanothus, known as buckbush seeds, are among those that respond to a brief period of high temperature called a heat shock. This is usually caused by a wildfire that burns away vegetation. The bare ground that remains is where the seed has space and soil nutrients to germinate.

WHICH WAY IS UP?

If a seed is upside down in dark soil, why doesn't it send its root up and its shoot down? It has tissues that sense light and gravity. The shoot grows against gravity (geotropism) and toward light (phototropism). Roots do the opposite.

A seedling extends its shoot toward the light.

OUT IN THE COLD

Some of the toughest habitats are cold regions at the poles and on mountains. Yet even in these areas, flowers can grow.

COPING WITH THE COLD

Some plants have features that help them survive in low temperatures. The leaves are covered with hairs that protect the insides from frost damage and reduce water loss. This stops the leaves of evergreen plants from drying out in the winter, when the soil is frozen and the roots cannot absorb water.

BEARBERRY

Alpine bearberry provides useful nourishment for many animals—including bears.

ALPINE MEADOW

The alpine (mountain) habitat comes to colorful life in late spring. Flowers known as ephemerals grow quickly, taking advantage of the short summer's warmth and long hours of daylight. The flowers make seeds before the cold and darkness return.

LOW CUSHIONS

The low, spreading shape of some flowers helps them in extreme conditions. This shape keeps most of the plant out of cold, drying winds. Many trees in cold regions are small and stunted for this reason. Flowers form low, clumped, shapes, known as a cushion habit. The plants are close together to support and protect one another.

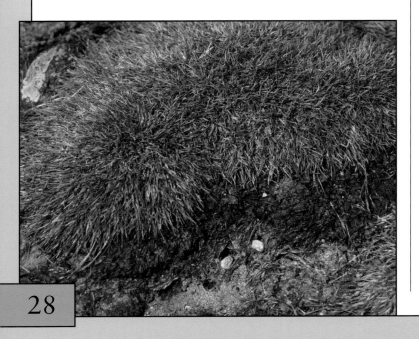

ARCTIC GRASS

Grasses of the far north often grow in clumps or thick mats. In severe weather, the outermost stems may die, but the inner ones are protected. Next year new shoots emerge from the middle of the clump.

SMALL TREES

Trees that have adapted to cold include rowans, also known as mountain ash. Chinese rowan (above) has white berries. On European rowan, the berries are red (above right). In exposed areas with strong winds, the Arctic willow (right) may only be 1 foot (30 cm) tall.

MOUNTAIN BLOOMS

Delicate flowering plants can grow on high mountains, but their flowers may only last a short time. In Europe, edelweiss (above) has hairy white leaves in a star shape around small yellow flowers. It is protected by law in many areas. Alpine clover (below) is found in the European Alps and the mountains of the western U.S. This perennial has a deep taproot to take up nutrients and water from the poor soil.

SURVIVING THE WINTER

Flowering plants are important food for animals in cold regions, including caribou, voles, and lemmings. These creatures paw away the snow to get at the greenery beneath. The plants survive better under the snow, which works as a blanket to protect them from icy winds.

Lemmings dig tunnels under the snow so they can continue to nibble plants through the winter.

The Arctic hare gnaws the twigs and roots of trees and woody shrubs, such as heathers. It also feasts on berries and other fruits.

Trees that are woody flowering plants are the main inhabitants of many broad-leaved woodlands, forests, and rain forests.

FOREST GUARDIANS

In areas with mild climates, a single tree can be host to more than a thousand species of animals. Through the seasons, the tree provides food in the form of buds, leaves, flowers, and acorn fruits. It gives shelter from cold winds in the winter and from the hot sun in the summer. Squirrels and birds nest in the branches, and foxes and bears make dens among the roots.

BEATING THE LEAVES

By late spring, when the trees have produced their leaves, the woodland floor is cast into a deep shade. Plants such as bluebells (above), primroses (below left), and trillium (bottom) flower early in the spring, before the leaves emerge. Bluebells are perennials that grow from bulbs in the soil. The food stored in the bulbs during the previous year allows the plants to get a head start growing from seeds. Primroses spread by underground stems called rhizomes.

CREEPERS

Creepers, vines, and lianas have long, flexible stems that rely on other plants for support. They wrap around trunks and branches. They include woodbine honeysuckles (right) and clematis.

SELF-DEFENSE

Flowering plants have many ways to defend themselves against plant-eating animals. Some produce chemical substances that give them a foul taste, warning animals that they are poisonous. Another type of chemical

defense is tiny stinging hairs, such as in nettles. Physical protection includes sharp spikes, prickles, and thorns.

Stinging nettles (left) got their name from the pain caused by touching them. The chemicals are released from tiny hairs. Acacias and other thornbushes have stiff, sharp spines (above).

TROPICAL FORESTS

Trees in the tropics support an even greater range of life. Species tend to be scattered through the tropics rather than growing in same-species groups. Many are evergreen, losing a few leaves constantly throughout the year.

LEAF LITTER

Fallen leaves form a layer called leaf litter (below). This provides tiny animals, molds, and fungi with nutrients, which they turn into soil for new plants.

IN THE RAIN FOREST

Flowering plants have many ways of living in the rain forest (above). The strangler fig (inset, top) wraps woody stems around a tree, stealing its nutrients and eventually killing it. Epiphytes (right) grow on other plants but get their nutrients from other sources.

GRASSLANDS

In places where the climate is too dry for trees, but too moist for a desert, grasses grow. These flowering plants support a huge variety of wildlife.

MONOCOTS

Grasses and similar plants are in the monocotyledon group of angiosperms. A typical grass plant has a tangle of small roots and hollow upright stems from which the long, slim leaves grow. These blades lengthen at their bases rather than at their tips. They can cope with being grazed (eaten) by animals at the tips, leaving the bases to grow undamaged.

BLADES
Some grasses have horizontal stems called blades on the ground, while the leaves are upright. This is the opposite from the way most flowering plants are structured.

POPULAR GRASS
Up to 10 feet (3 m) tall, pampas grass from South America is grown worldwide for its large feathery flowers and seedheads.

WIDE-OPEN PLAINS
Vast grasslands or plains are on most continents. There are steppes in Asia (above), savannas in Africa (far right), prairies in North America (inset, right), and pampas in South America. Each region has its own grass species. However, many of these natural grasslands have been replaced by farm crops, which are also grasses.

GRASS FLOWERS

Almost all grasses are wind-pollinated, so their flowers lack bright petals, strong scents, and sweet nectar. The flowers are in groups, known as spikes, at the stem tip. A spike consists of several spikelets, and each of these has small individual flowers called florets. The floret has scalelike glumes at its base. Grass flowerheads are mostly green or brown. They are packed together in wheat (above) and more spaced out along the stems in fescue (right).

BRILLIANT BAMBOO

The biggest grasses are bamboos. Like tree trunks, their hollow stems are stiffened with woody fibers. Some species grow to heights of 130 feet (40 m). There are more than 1,000 species, and most are found in tropical regions.

A bamboo stem is divided into sections by cross-walls, called nodes (left), where leaves grow. Some species do not flower for many years. Then all the plants in an area produce flowers at the same time (below). This can greatly affect animals such as the giant panda (above), which eats little else.

GRASS SEEDS

Known as grains, grass seeds are packed with stored food for the embryo plants inside. This makes them nourishing for animals and people as well.

GRASSLAND WILDLIFE

Animals that eat grasses and other low plants are known as grazers. On the open grasslands in Africa, grazers include antelopes, gazelles, giraffes, and zebras. In North America, grazers such as cattle and bison roam the grasslands.

WETLAND PLANTS

Some flowering plants are at home in the wet conditions of swamps, marshes, bogs, rivers, and lakes. One species often takes over an entire area.

DIFFICULT HABITATS

Flowering plants can have difficulty living in wetlands. The water may rise during heavy rains, then seep away and leave the ground dry during a heat wave. Thick mud often builds up and chokes plant roots. The stagnant (still) water has little oxygen, which plants need to survive.

Wetland flowering plants grow at various depths. There are marginals around the water's edge, emergents in the shallow water, long-stemmed plants with floating leaves in deep water, and floaters in the open water.

WINTER FLOOD

Rising water levels in winter, a result of more rain and less heat for drying, mean that most wetland flowers will die, leaving only taller grasses and trees.

REED BEDS

Reeds are types of grasses. They spread rapidly by thick underground stems called rhizomes. In rivers their stems slow the water current and trap particles of mud and silt. The reed bed gradually spreads, but it may be swept away by a flood. Papyrus reed beds often build up along the Nile River in Egypt.

AERIAL ROOTS

Coastal mangroves (left) are among the few flowering plants that can cope with salty water. They send up aerial roots from the thick mud to take in oxygen.

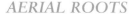

34

Growing at heights of more than 3,300 feet (1,000 m) in western Europe, bog asphodel's yellow flowers (below) bring splashes of color in midsummer.

WATER BLOOMS

One of the best-known wetland flower families is the water lilies, with more than 70 species. The rounded, floating leaves grow on stems up to 10 feet (3 m) long and are rooted in the mud. The flowers open only in bright weather.

MARSH MARIGOLD

One of the first flowers to appear in early spring, the marsh marigold (below) may continue blooming until midsummer.

LARGE LILIES

The leaves of the largest water lily, Victoria amazonica from South America (above), are broad enough to support the weight of a small child. It was named after Queen Victoria of Great Britain.

CARNIVOROUS PLANTS

The decay of dead plants happens slowly in waterlogged, low-oxygen soil. This leads to a buildup of acidic chemicals. This means the soil lacks nutrients. Carnivorous plants get around the problem by eating meat. They feed on insects and other small creatures that become trapped in their leaves.

The hinged leaf of a Venus flytrap (right) snaps shut, trapping insects that touch hairs in its middle.

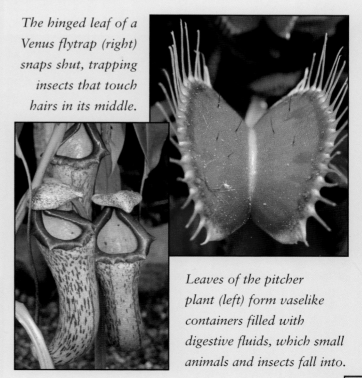

Sundews (left) catch their prey with drops of thick, sticky liquid on their leaf hairs.

Leaves of the pitcher plant (left) form vaselike containers filled with digestive fluids, which small animals and insects fall into.

DESERTS AND DROUGHTS

One of the biggest challenges for flowering plants is taking in enough water. Yet flowering plants manage to survive droughts.

XEROPHYTES
Plants that cope with aridity (a lack of water) are known as xerophytes. Many are succulents—they store water in their leaves, stems, or roots. These plants include many species of cactuses and bromeliads. Desert trees may drop their leaves in the dry season to prevent continuing water loss.

AFTER THE RAIN
Within days after rain falls in a desert, flowers such as desert poppies (inset, above right) carpet the once bare ground with color. Ephemerals (right) germinate, bloom, and make seeds before drought sets in again.

PRICKLY WARNING
The aloe group contains about 400 species of flowering plants from Africa. Most have spokelike rosettes of thick, fleshy leaves with spines or thorns.

SAVING WATER

Another way for plants to conserve water is through the use of stomata. These parts are set into grooves of leaves and slow the loss of water. A thick waxy layer on the leaf, called the cuticle, makes it more waterproof. Desert plants often have wide or deep root systems. Some tree roots go down as much as 50 feet (15 m), where the subsoil and rocks almost always have water.

GUM TREES OF THE OUTBACK

Australia has more than 700 species of eucalypts. They are also called gum trees because they ooze a thick, sticky fluid from cracks or holes in the bark. This prevents pests and diseases from getting in. Many have flaky or stringy bark.

LIVING STONES

Various species of lithops are also known as living stones or stone plants. Their color makes them look like pebbles, helping them avoid the attention of animals.

DESERT CACTUSES

With more than 2,000 species, the cactus family is most common in North and South America. Most have swollen green stems for photosynthesis and water storage. They have few leaves, sharp spines, and often very deep roots. Some species go 50 years between flowering periods.

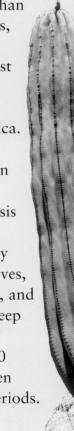

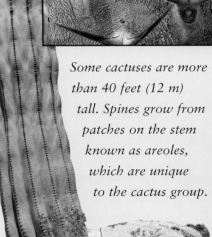

Some cactuses are more than 40 feet (12 m) tall. Spines grow from patches on the stem known as areoles, which are unique to the cactus group.

It is hard to imagine life without flowering plants. They give us food, drink, clothes, building materials, and many other products.

FOOD FROM PLANTS

Much of the world depends on food from the grass family, especially grains, such as wheat, barley, rye, and rice. Fruits vary from common apples and oranges to less known azaras and zabalas. There are thousands of kinds of nuts and berries. There is also a wide variety of vegetables, including potatoes and greens, such as lettuces, and lesser known kinds, such as rutabaga, yacona, kohlrabi, and salsify.

ORCHARDS AND HOME GARDENS

Orchards (above) are large areas of trees that produce fruit, including apples, pears, oranges, cherries, and olives. The trees are pruned regularly by trimming their branches so that they stay healthy and continue to produce good crops. Many people enjoy growing their own fruits and vegetables, such as lettuce (left), at home.

FARMLAND

More land is devoted to crops—especially for grains, such as wheat and barley (above)—than to any other human use. Some crops are grown as food for livestock. More specialized crops include cumin and peppercorns (left).

MODERN MEDICINES

More than half of all modern medical drugs originally came from flowering plants. One of the best known is aspirin, which was first prepared from the bark of willow trees (left). Research is being done with rare plants from remote areas to see whether they have medical uses.

HERBAL REMEDIES

Natural herbs, such as ginger, have been used for thousands of years to treat various ailments. They can be made into drinks, powders, or pills, or mixed with foods. Treating illness by inhaling the scents from plant oils is called aromatherapy.

Gingerroot

Herbs are sold around the world. Herb stores are especially popular in Japan, Italy, and China.

OILS AND AROMAS

Flowering plants produce herbs and spices, such as vanilla, ginger, and oregano, that are used in cooking. Plant oils, such as sunflower, palm, soya, and olive, are widely used. Apart from edible products, there are hundreds of flower-based scents, including mint, rose, honeysuckle, and passionflower.

BUILDING MATERIALS

Plants are used for many kinds of construction materials other than wood. The stems of grasses and reeds are laid as thatched roofs (right). In Asia, bamboo stems are used as scaffolding poles (below), as well as the framework of buildings.

FUEL CROPS

Sugarcane (above), sugar beets, and corn provide ethanol used in fuels for our cars and trucks. Another source of biofuels is oily plants, such as oil palm and canola.

39

THE FLOWER BUSINESS

A part from supplying useful products, plants are valued for their beauty and variety.

HORTICULTURE

The science of growing plants, especially on a large scale, is known as horticulture. To develop new breeds and varieties, experts use many methods, including artificial pollination and vegetative propagation by cuttings. Scientists are continually developing new techniques, such as genetic modification, to breed plants.

FLOWER SHOWS

Horticulturalists gather to show their new breeds at huge events, such as the Chelsea Flower Show in London, England.

IMPORTANT FEATURES

When trying to breed new flower varieties, the color, shape, and appearance of the flowers are important. The plant should be easy to grow. It should also make plenty of seeds and be resistant to disease. Otherwise mass production will be too expensive.

SACRED FLOWER

The lotus (left) grows in a similar way to the water lily, but it is from a different plant family. It has been worshipped in several parts of the world, especially Egypt, as shown on ancient carvings (right).

SELECTIVE BREEDING

For centuries plant experts have selected plants with certain features and bred them to make new varieties. The features are usually the result of mutations—changes in the genes that occur in plants that reproduce sexually.

INSTANT CHANGE

Selective breeding can take many life cycles over several years to produce new plant types. In genetic modification, new genes can be added in one generation that will affect future generations. However, genetic engineers must be sure that new gene combinations do not turn plants into "superweeds" that can cause problems in nature.

GENETIC ENGINEERING

Genes from other species can be introduced into a plant in the laboratory, resulting in what is called a transgenic strain.

DEADLY POISONS

For thousands of years, people have known about the poisonous effects of certain plants. The plants have sometimes been used to commit murder. Well-known species that are poisonous if eaten include hemlock, wolfsbane, laburnum, oleander, and deadly nightshade. Poison ivy causes severe skin rash.

The deadly nightshade was named for its fatal effect.

Socrates, a famous philosopher of ancient Greece (above left), was condemned to an agonizing death by drinking poisonous plant juices, probably made from hemlock (left).

BIO-DETECTORS

A type of thale cress was genetically altered to change color when it grows in soil containing traces of certain explosives. This could make it useful for detecting land mines and other explosives.

41

FLOWERS UNDER THREAT

With each year that passes, more and more of nature is under threat. Flowering plants are no exception. Rare flowering plants and trees are at great risk.

GROWING PROBLEM
More than 10,000 angiosperms are on the list of threatened species. But many other species have not yet been studied thoroughly, so the actual number of plants at risk is probably much higher. For example, there is only one wild specimen of the tree *Pennantia baylisiana* left in the world.

PINK IN PERIL
Cheddar pink grows wild only in one gorge in Somerset, England, and is protected by law.

SO MANY THREATS
The main threat to flowering plants is habitat loss. Construction takes over wild places to build farms, roads, and buildings. Other problems include pollution, the cutting down of trees for timber, the collecting of rare flowers, the introduction of foreign species to an area, and global warming.

HABITAT LOSS

In several tropical regions, especially southeast Asia, oil palm plantations (below) are taking over natural forest landscapes (left). Oil from the fruits (right) is used for many purposes, from cooking to making soaps and cosmetics that are used all over the world. Meanwhile the local plants and animals, such as orangutans, are quickly disappearing.

FLOWER THIEVES

Despite wildlife laws, plant collectors still dig up rare flowers, such as slipper orchids (right). This puts the flowers at even greater risk. Growing plants in cultivation helps to avoid the problem.

RARE BUT COMMON

Some angiosperms may seem common because they are grown in our backyards, parks, and greenhouses. But they may be especially rare or even absent in nature, a condition known as "extinct in the wild." Two examples are Cosmos atrosanguineus *(above) and* Franklinia alatamaha *(right).*

PROBLEM WEEDS

A weed is a plant that grows where it is not wanted. Various flowering plants introduced to a new region have no natural predators, such as herbivores or diseases. This allows them to spread out of control.

Kudzu is a climbing vine that grows in eastern Asia. In the 1870s, it was brought to North America as a decorative plant. It spread unchecked and choked large areas of natural habitat (above). Thistles (right) are another species that causes problems when introduced to new areas.

POLLEN PROBLEM

The alula in Hawaii is one of the world's rarest plants, with fewer than 50 specimens in the wild. The animal best adapted to pollinate it, a particular kind of hawk moth, recently became extinct. Now plant experts have to do this task.

43

CLASSIFICATION OF LIFE

Scientists classify living things depending on how their features and the parts inside them compare with those of other living things. Flowering plants (angiosperms) share one main feature—their seeds are enclosed. But there are many groups, from delicate herbs to massive trees. Their similarities and differences show how flowering plants have evolved around the world over millions of years.

The main groups of living things are known as domains. The next groups are usually kingdom, phylum (division), class, order, family, genus, and species. To see how this system works, follow the example on page 45 of how the dog rose *Rosa canina* is classified in the division Magnoliophyta.

BIOLOGICAL CLASSIFICATION: DOMAINS

BACTERIA

 Single-celled prokaryotes, found in most places on Earth

ARCHAEA

 Single-celled prokaryotes, many surviving in extreme conditions

EUKARYA

KINGDOMS

 PROTISTA: Single-celled eukaryotes, with some simple multicelled forms

 FUNGI: Multicelled life-forms that digest their food externally

 PLANTAE: Multicelled life-forms that obtain energy by photosynthesis

 ANIMALIA: Multicelled life-forms that get their energy by taking in food